Printed in Great Britain
by Amazon

69922753R00059